Climate Change

A Simple, Flexible,

And

Profitable Approach

By Gary Keir

Published by: Inspired Press Publisher

9394 Greenery Court

Loveland, OH 45140

www.inspiredpresspublisher.com

Disclaimer

No part of this publication may be reproduced, stored in a retrieval system, or transmitted in any form or by any means, electronic, mechanical, photocopying, recording, scanning or otherwise, except as permitted by the author.

Limit of Liability/Disclaimer of Warranty: While the author and publisher have made every effort to ensure that the information in this book was correct at press time, the author and publisher do not assume and hereby disclaim any liability to any party for any loss, damage, or disruption caused by errors or omissions, whether such errors or omissions result from negligence, accident, or any other cause.

The book contains information about climate control and new solutions. The information is not advice, and should not be treated as such.

You must not rely on the information in the book as an alternative to legal or financial advice from an appropriately qualified professional. If you have any specific questions about any legal or financial matter you should consult an appropriately qualified professional.

Gary Keir Bio

Gary was born and raised in Pittsburgh PA and worked in the family roofing and heating business. It is here that he was first exposed to the benefits of energy efficiency. He later became a biologist and worked on  the Marathon Battery Superfund site and the Westway Fisheries study. For the past 20 years he has been solving problems as an IT contractor involved in programming, business analysis, and project management. His interest in environmental issues has led him to become a trip leader for Sierra Club Outings. He leads backpacking and rafting trips in arctic Alaska. He came up with the concept of Carbon Xprint because he felt overwhelmed by the problem of climate change and that his options to do anything about it were extremely limited. He currently resides in New York City.

Table of Contents

Simple Physics

There is so much talk about climate change, greenhouse gases, and global warming. It can seem so confusing. What is it really? I hope this analogy can help explain global warming even to those who have an aversion to science. Think of a stove that has been turned on. When we put a pot on the stove, the pot absorbs some of that heat and it gets and stays hot, but the handle of the pot stays cool enough to pick up the pot without burning your hand because it does not absorb the heat. The sun heats up the surface of the earth like the surface of a stove. We all know how on a hot summer day the sun can make the sidewalk or the sand on a beach so hot that it is difficult to walk on in our bare feet. Greenhouse gases above the earth's surface are like the pot sitting on the stove. The greenhouse gases absorb the heat so they get warm and they stay warm. The other gases are like the handle of the pot. They let the heat pass through and out into space. The more pots that we have on the stove, the hotter it will be in the kitchen. The more greenhouse gases we have in the air, the warmer it will be on earth. It is simply the physical properties of the gases in our air and their ability to either absorb heat or to let it pass through.

These greenhouse gases are not new and they are actually very important. They absorb enough heat to keep the earth in a temperature range that we can live in. Global Warming and Climate Change occur when they get out of balance. To use the analogy above, when there are too many pots on the stove, the kitchen gets too hot.

So, how then, do greenhouse gasses get out of balance?

Fossil Fuels

If it weren't for fossil fuels, we would have slaughtered all of the whales for oil and cut down all of the trees for industry, cooking, and heating our homes and businesses. They are miracle compounds. One gallon of gasoline can move a one-ton hunk of metal 30 miles with an engine that is only 25% efficient. Unfortunately like some other materials such as asbestos, that perform as well, these compounds have serious unwanted side effects. The main chemical element in fossil fuels is carbon. All of this carbon in fossil fuels has been buried in the ground. When we take them out of the ground and we burn them, the carbon combines with oxygen in the air to make carbon dioxide. Carbon dioxide is a gas that absorbs and holds on to heat more than the other gases. So now we have taken carbon that has been buried in the ground and we have put it into the air as a greenhouse gas. This changes the balance of greenhouse gases in the air. When we find out that some of our high performing products such as asbestos, DDT, PCBs, and even tobacco have the potential to do more harm than good, we have eliminated them from our environment and moved on. We used to think that meat and potatoes were the best meal or fuel for our bodies. It is a great meal, but we know now that too much of that diet has unwanted side effects and we have accepted that we should modify our diets. We know that using fossil fuels is currently and will continue to do harm. Why is it so difficult to accept and move forward to a new hopeful and safe reality?

Moving Forward

When there is a change in technology, which is inevitable and how our economy grows, many people lose their jobs. For example, the Information Age brought huge changes in the way we run our offices, processes, and factories. While some, such as I, were given opportunities in the new and growing industry, many others were automated out of their jobs. As a society, we are not good at retraining and giving displaced hard working people opportunities in the changing workplace - especially as they get older. Identities are often tied to professions and professions are often tied to towns and even cities. When the jobs leave, workers and towns can lose not only what they do but also who they are. For them, it's more than just economics, it's about self-worth and self-identity. It is not hard to see why people in the fossil fuel business would be resistant to change. But, what about the rest of us? Why are we resistant to change?

Do Unto Others

We are lucky to be alive in this day and age. We live in a society that offers many benefits to enjoy. We are warm in winter and cool in summer. We can get around easier and faster than in any time in history. Fresh vegetables are available year round. Communication and entertainment are literally at our fingertips. The energy choices that make this society possible; electricity that turns on our lights and powers up the internet, the fuels that move our cars and planes, warm our water and heat our homes, businesses, and public facilities come from the burning of fossil fuels. However, if we continue to burn these fuels, people will be hurt. If not now, then sometime in the future. How would you feel if someone else's actions caused your home to flood or your fields to dry up? Most of us live by the golden rule "do unto others as you would have them do unto you". No one wants to believe that the simple act of going about our daily lives will cause somebody harm.

We did not create this fossil fuel dependent society, we inherited it. It will cause human suffering. We do not have to defend it. It is our responsibility to accept the consequences of what we inherited by moving forward to reverse this inevitability before it's too late. How do we make a change? How do we move forward?

Essential Components

To achieve the goal of reducing greenhouse gasses, a successful carbon reduction strategy will have to contain the following components:

Measurability

"What gets measured gets managed" ~ Peter Drucker

We need to see where we are, how far we have come, and how far we need to go.

Simplicity

"Simplicity is the ultimate sophistication" ~ Leonardo Da Vinci

A successful strategy will be one that we all can understand. To get more companies and individuals involved, the strategy must be something that is easy to do and not too different from something that they know how to do already. It must be a shallow learning curve.

Engagement

"Tell me and I'll forget; show me and I may remember; involve me and I'll understand" ~ Chinese proverb

We are all responsible for climate change. For all of us to be a part of correcting climate change, we need a mechanism that allows all of us to be engaged.

Flexibility

"Do what you can, with what you have, where you are."
~ Theodore Roosevelt

Not all of us have the same options. Not all of us can install solar collectors or change the insulation in our walls. A successful strategy will allow people and businesses to do what they can with what they have.

Profits

"Business is all about solving people's problems - at a profit." ~ Paul Marsden

In the end solving climate change is about money. The political reality is that we will not be able to tax and punish to change behavior. Sacrifice will work with only a small group of people for a limited time. We need a carrot and not a stick - strategy where not only society gains but the individual gains as well.

Positivity

"Attitude is a little thing that makes a big difference." ~ Winston Churchill

So many strategies and attitudes toward correcting climate change focus on the negative. A defensive stance to ward off impending doom does not work because it is a doom that can be difficult to visualize. A successful strategy is devoid of threats. It will employ being on the offensive, looking forward and focusing on the positive. It will focus on creating a better future and building a new energy infrastructure. Nothing motivates like progress.

Carbon Xprint

The amount of greenhouse gases produced by the burning of fossil fuels as we go about our daily lives is called our carbon footprints. What kind of changes can we make to reduce these carbon footprints? There is simply not enough space for all of us to go back to a lifestyle where we live off the land and live off the grid. Sacrificing the comforts of our society is not an option. What actions can we then take? Some actions are easy: wasting less by reusing and recycling, walking more, adjusting the thermostat, and using public transportation when possible. These actions may make some positive impact, but the majority of our carbon footprints remain. Our energy choices are limited and for the most part, out of our control. Right now, it may not be possible or feasible to change the insulation in our walls or install new windows to make our homes and businesses more energy efficient. Our locations may not lend themselves to renewable energy such as solar panels or wind mills. There seems to be little we can do to make a substantial change to reverse the inevitable catastrophes that seem imminent. Though it appears overwhelming, but perhaps a new approach can help us move forward. We need something that will allow us to be a part of the change when our options are limited, something that does not require punishment and sacrifice but offers rewards. Carbon Xprint is designed to entice and engage all individuals and businesses to reduce their carbon footprints when their other options are limited. It is designed to be measurable – taking action one ton at a time; simple – as easy as going to a bank; engaging – individuals to major corporations can become invested in correcting climate change; flexible – allowing anyone to do what they can with what they have; profitable – because money is returned plus interest; and positive – focus on creating a better future. Carbon Xprint helps solve two of climate change's biggest challenges, the need to take action for our greenhouse gases and the need for investment in a new energy infrastructure. How does it work?

How it Works

Carbon Xprint is very simple. It works exactly like a traditional savings bond or a CD but it has the added qualitative benefit of being a socially-responsible investment in renewable energy and energy efficiency. In addition, it certifies in a measurable way that you (or your company) is doing all you can to help counteract climate change.

Here is how it works. A company, building owner, or individual calculates their carbon footprint in tons of greenhouse gases. Note: The following is the EPA website that can assist with the calculation.

http://www.epa.gov/climatechange/ghgemissions/ind-calculator.html

According to the EPA, an average one-person household produces 10 tons of greenhouse gases per year. When they know what their carbon footprint is, they then go to a financial institution, in person or online, and purchase a Carbon Xprint CD. The Carbon Xprint CD is based on the price of one ton of greenhouse gas. Let us say the price of one ton of greenhouse gas is $30. A business or person that has a carbon footprint of 10 tons would purchase a Carbon Xprint CD for $300. The business or person is then certified that they took action for their carbon footprint. The financial institution takes that money and lends it out to energy efficiency and renewable energy projects. These projects reduce the amount of greenhouse gases that go into the air. The institution will make money on that loan. At the end of the term the Carbon Xprint CD holder will get their money back plus interest.

Measure your carbon footprint in tons of greenhouse gases.

Buy Carbon Xprint CDs.

Certifies action taken for greenhouse gases.

Loans to efficiency and renewable energy projects.

At the end of the term the Carbon Xprint CD holder gets their money back plus interest.

2050

The UN's Intergovernmental Panel on Climate Change states that it is crucial that we keep average global surface temperatures from rising more than 2 degrees Celsius. Going beyond this temperature means risking "high-impact" changes such as the melting of the Greenland Ice Shield. Carbon Xprint is designed to increase investment in renewable energy and energy efficiency. How much investment is needed?

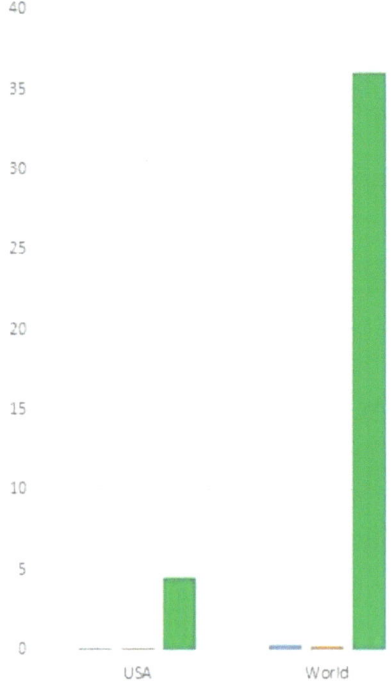

Current Investment and Needed Investment in $ Trillions

Energy Efficiency Investment ■ Renewable Energy Investment ■ Investment Needed to meet 2050 Goal

The amount of investment needed to meet the goal of keeping global temperatures below a 2 degree Celsius rise by the year 2050 and the current amount of investment in energy efficiency and renewable energy. According to the Rocky Mountain Institute, the $4.5 trillion investment in the US would yield $9.5 trillion in savings. A net savings of $5 trillion.

Carbon Xprint is also a process to allow us to take action for our carbon footprint in tons of greenhouse gases. How much do we have to reduce our carbon footprint?

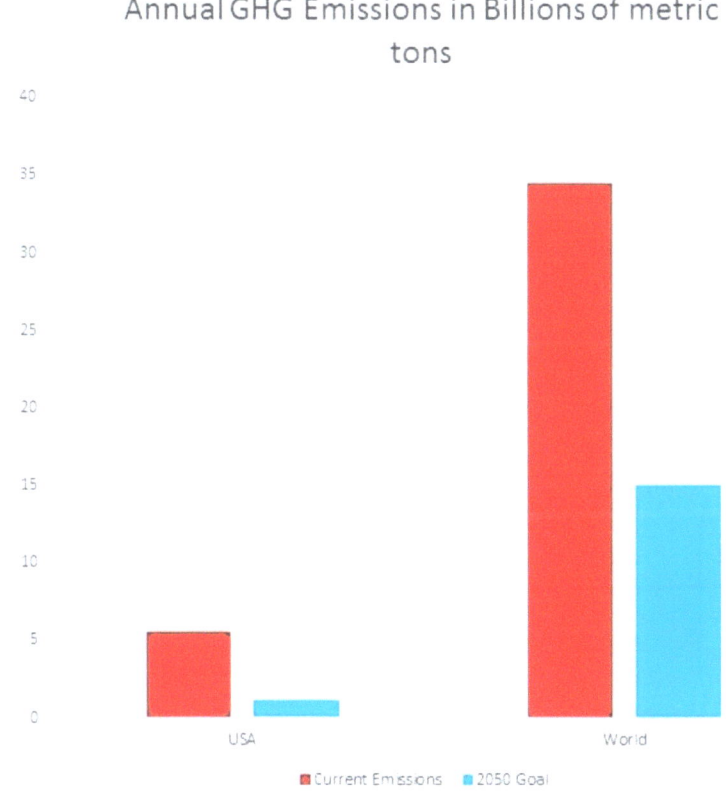

Annual GHG Emissions in Billions of metric tons

The amount of greenhouse gases (GHG) released into the air today and the 2050 target amount to keep global temperatures below a 2 degree Celsius rise.

Other Strategies

The other strategies to reduce greenhouse gases currently being used and considered are Cap and Trade, Renewable Energy Credits, and the Carbon Tax.

Carbon Tax is a tax levied on the greenhouse gas potential of fuels. The money collected from this strategy would go to governments.

Cap and Trade sets emissions limits for large scale emitters. Companies that emit less than their limit can sell allowances to companies that exceed their limit. For example, the government sets the amount of greenhouse gases that Company A can put into the air at 10 tons and the government sets the same level for Company B. At the end of the year Company A put only 8 tons of greenhouse gases into the air while Company B put 12 tons of greenhouse gases into the air. Company A is two tons below the limit set by the government and Company B is two tons above the limit. Through an elaborate trading system, Company A can sell an allowance of two tons of greenhouse gases to Company B so they will both end up with a limit of 10 tons and meet the government requirements.

Renewable Energy Credits are a production subsidy for grid-tied renewable energy. The purchaser receives only a certificate. For example, Company A wants to show its customers that it is a 'green' company. Company A looks into solar energy but is located in a shady area. Company B is in a sunny area and puts solar collectors on its warehouse. It produces more electricity than it can use so it sells the extra electricity back to the utility. Company B can also produce a certificate stating that it sold so many kilowatt hours of electricity generated from a renewable source to the utility. Company A can buy those certificates and state to their customers that they are being 'green'.

The price of a ton of greenhouse gases in Cap and Trade and the price of a Renewable Energy Credit can vary not only over time but also from region to region. These systems also require complex trading structures. To change behavior, the approach of these three strategies is either punishment for actions taken in the present and/or reward for actions taken in the past. When a company cannot make an imposed limit, these approaches make it harder for the company to achieve those limits. With Cap and trade and Renewable Energy Credits money is paid to existing renewable energy and efficiency. A better approach would be to make it easier for companies to achieve imposed limits. Money paid would be better spent in creating additional renewable energy and energy efficiency. A better approach would be to reward action in the present to create a better future. These three approaches are defensive postures. People can more easily support an approach that is on the offensive, progressing, building, creating, and moving forward than an approach that is defensive and holding its ground. Being a part of progress enhances motivation. This is the approach of Carbon Xprint. To reward action today and get the money to where it is needed to do the most good, creating energy efficiency and renewable energy.

Other Strategies

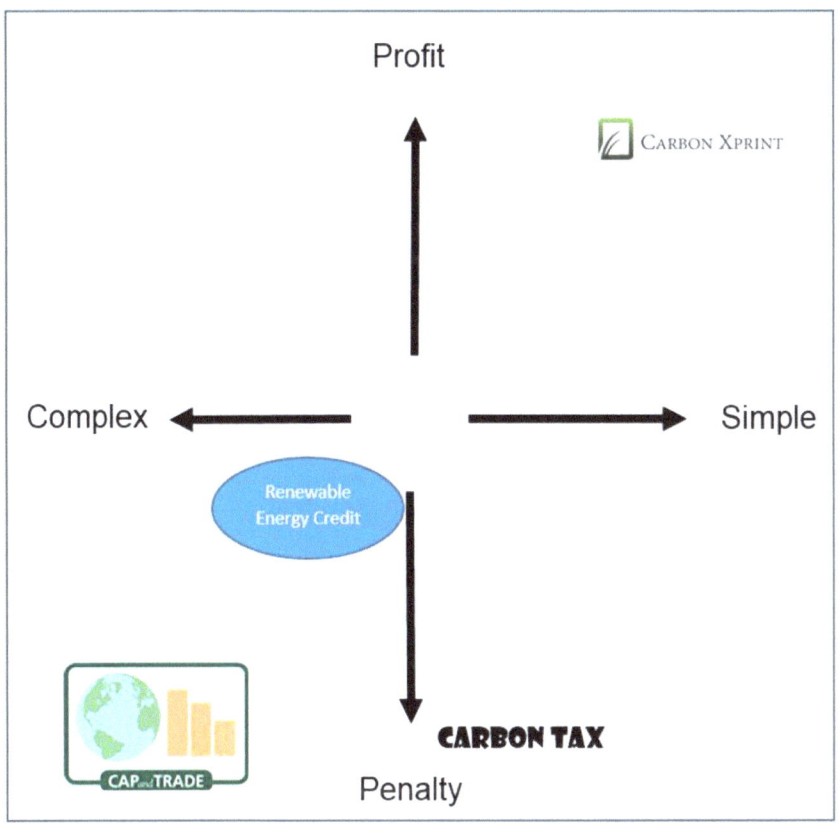

Benefits for Individuals

- Since we are all responsible for climate change, we can all make a profit by being part of the solution.
- A person could offset their carbon footprint with Carbon Xprint CDs, and then donate those bonds to the fire department, library, or church as part of their charitable giving, thus fulfilling two missions with the same dollar.
- Carbon Xprint Bonds relieve the feeling of helplessness that many feel when facing the problem of climate change.
- It is helping the environment without sacrifice. Xprint Bond holders get their money back, plus interest.
- Carbon Xprint CDs can allow options. If a homeowner plans to make a major efficiency or renewable energy improvement some years in the future but wants to take environmental responsibility in the current year, they could purchase Carbon Xprint CDs now, and then use the capital and interest earned to finance the project sometime down the road – like a Christmas Club for energy efficiency.
- Carbon Xprint Bonds could be used in a 401K or 529 College Savings Plans.
- Carbon Xprint CDs sold by banks are FDIC insured.
- The energy infrastructure will have to change sooner or later. Might as well be part of the solution and make money from it.
- Carbon Xprint CDs help leave the world a better place for your children and grandchildren.

Benefits for Companies

- Carbon Xprint yield profits. Other greenhouse gas reduction strategies are penalties.
- Carbon Xprint could help a company in the supply chain of large retailers and manufacturers meet stronger sustainability requirements and thus remain competitive.
- Carbon Xprint CDs are not subject to the changing winds of government programs.
- Carbon Xprint provides stability in the price of carbon. The bonds are not subject to the volatility of the carbon trading markets.
- Carbon Xprint CDs could be administered by the commercial banking system — an infrastructure that is well established.
- Carbon Xprint can allow options. If your company plans to make a major efficiency or renewable energy improvement some years in the future but wants to show environmental responsibility in the current fiscal year, it could purchase Carbon Xprint Bonds now, and then use the capital and interest earned to finance the project in a future fiscal year. Your company demonstrates sustainability today with funds for efficiency and renewable energy down the road.
- High sustainable businesses are more profitable than low sustainable businesses. More companies are filing sustainability reports. Carbon Xprint Bonds are a tangible demonstration of sustainability.
- Carbon Xprint Bonds provide a convenient method for any size or type of business to demonstrate sustainability.

- An entity could offset CO2E emissions with Carbon Xprint Bonds, then donate those bonds as part of that entity's charitable giving, thus fulfilling two missions with the same dollar.
- Carbon Xprint CDs could be incorporated into your customer loyalty programs.
- Renewable energy and efficiency projects are not only good for the planet but they also reduce operating costs.
- Universities could offset their carbon footprint by having their endowment fund purchase Carbon Xprint Bonds.